essence of
seashore

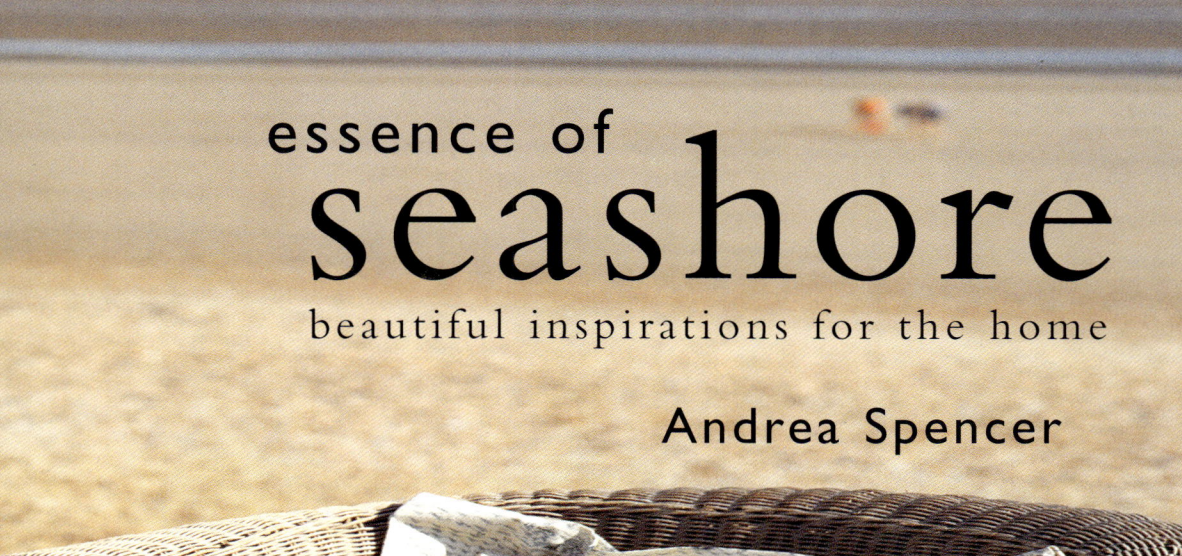

essence of
seashore

beautiful inspirations for the home

Andrea Spencer

LORENZ BOOKS

First published by Lorenz Books in 2002

Lorenz Books is an imprint of
Anness Publishing Limited
Hermes House
88–89 Blackfriars Road
London SE1 8HA

Published in the USA by Lorenz Books,
Anness Publishing Inc, 27 West 20th Street,
New York, NY 10011

www.lorenzbooks.com

This edition distributed in Canada by Raincoast Books,
9050 Shaughnessy Street, Vancouver, British Columbia V6P 6E5

A CIP catalogue record for this book
is available from the British Library

Publisher JOANNA LORENZ
Managing editor JUDITH SIMONS
Senior art manager CLARE REYNOLDS
Project editor SARAH AINLEY
Editorial reader JOY WOTTON
Indexer HELEN SNAITH
Designers LOUISE CLEMENTS and OPTA DESIGN
Photography SPIKE POWELL
Additional photography POLLY ELTES, MICHELLE GARRETT,
DEBBIE PATTERSON, GRAHAM RAE, JO WHITWORTH,
PETER WILLIAMS and STEVEN WOOSTER
Production controller CLAIRE RAE

1 3 5 7 9 10 8 6 4 2

PUBLISHER'S NOTE
A special thank you to Chris Richardson and Gill Alcock for allowing
their home to be photographed on pp25, 31 (top left), 43 (top right).

Contents

Introduction

ABOVE Smooth pebbles from the beach appear as objects of simple beauty in the home or garden.

AS THE PACE OF LIVING increases, so does the need to create a harmonious home environment. Seashore style fulfils such a need – its fresh minimal approach works well in any setting, traditional or modern. Its essence is the sea itself. To walk across the beach and dip your toes in the ocean is one of life's great joys. You enter a world of light, space and energy, where wind and waves create an ever-changing environment. Picking up a pebble, you marvel at its shape and, sensing it to be precious, slip it into a pocket. Squinting into a rock pool, you spy movement and are suddenly a child again. Seashore style can recall deep memories and recapture the invigorating sensation of well-being you experience by the sea.

BELOW Sun-bleached life belts can be incorporated in seaside interiors as decorative motifs.

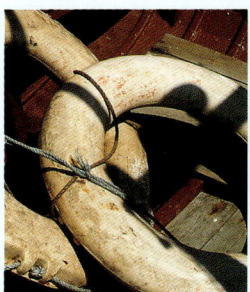

OPPOSITE PAGE Timeless elements of seashore style stir powerful feelings of freedom and harmony with nature and evoke memories of carefree holidays.

seashore pebbles boats driftwood mist shells waves

beach huts sand breakwater shingle rock pools coastline

Seashore Style

Wander along the shoreline and you'll find a beachcomber's treasure trove that provides an endless source of inspiration for decorative treatments.

ABOVE Shoreline finds such as faded floats and old fishing nets recall the seafaring life.

SEASHORE STYLE uses materials that improve with the passing of time, and furniture and furnishings that are simple, practical and, above all, comfortable. Seashore style is calm and easy on the eye. It provides a welcome antidote to life in the fast lane. It is all about appreciating the natural environment, taking the time to relax and savour the here-and-now aspects of life.

Matt, chalky seascape colours are important to the look, as are uneven surfaces and distressed patterns that evoke the ebb and flow of the sea along the shoreline. Wood and stone blend harmoniously with each other and with unpretentious canvas, calico and muslin.

Wicker, jute, raffia and rope can be combined with seashells and driftwood to give a balanced, homely living space and to provide a restful backdrop for day-to-day existence.

Genuine seashore style recreates the essential simplicity of ocean life. While it can be as basic as displaying your own beachcombing finds on a windowsill, you can take it further by drawing on classic maritime themes to decorate a room.

So take a stroll along the shore and seek your inspiration from nature's treasures at the water's edge. Use the colours, textures and gifts of the sea as creative themes to beautify your home and remind you of the happy, peaceful days you have spent beside the sea.

BELOW The resilient plants of clifftop and shore provide sculptural shapes in the garden.

sea breezes ice cream buoys starfish sand-dunes

Found objects need very little arranging – in fact, the simpler the better. Scoop up a handful of smooth pebbles and look closely at their varied colours and their intricate patterning and veining. Large worn stones look beautiful casually displayed on shelves, but they can also do duty as paperweights, doorstops or hearthside ornaments. Driftwood, worn smooth by the relentless pounding of sea waves, becomes sculpture for a window or mantelpiece, and larger pieces can be crafted into furniture. Take a closer look at the wonderful textures of rusting anchors and weathervanes. Collect seaworn shells and use them as a reminder of the patterns of nature that are the very essence of the seashore.

CLOCKWISE FROM ABOVE The subdued tones of sea–weathered materials such as painted metal, rope and wood are central colours in seashore style.

surf deck chairs flags life belts salt water fishing nets

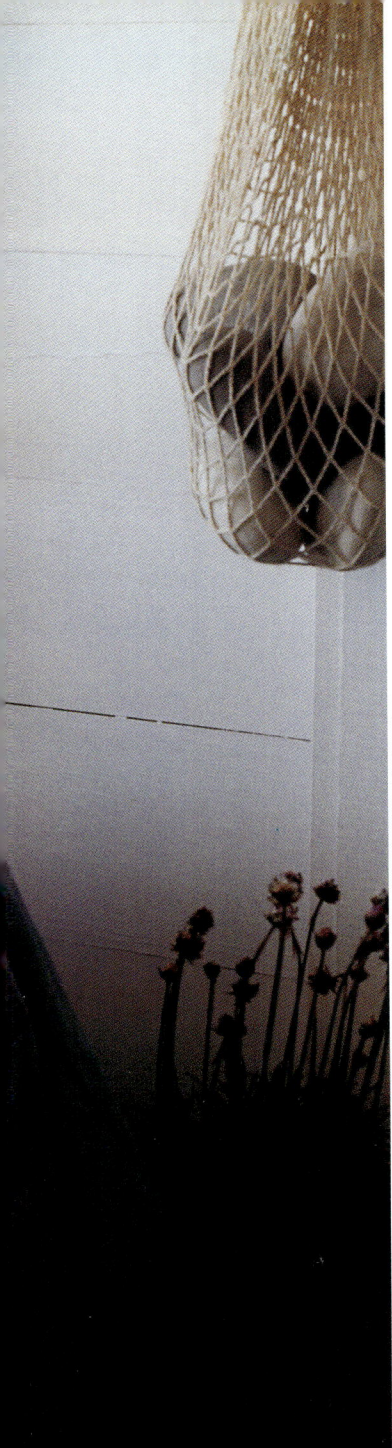

Marine Dining

LEISURELY MEALTIMES are the perfect way to savour good food and the company of family and friends. Introducing seashore style into kitchens and dining rooms will create an atmosphere of simplicity and comfort that provides the ideal setting for relaxed eating. On sunny days and warm evenings, take food outdoors and imagine yourself by the water's edge. Put up a beach parasol, or create a shady area with a canopy, and breathe in the fresh sea breeze.

ABOVE Fine china decorated with marine motifs adds novelty to the table.

LEFT A tiny beach hut verandah painted white is an idyllic setting for a leisurely summer meal. Choose bright checks and stripes for table linen, teamed with plain white enamelware for a fresh seaside feel.

Seaside Kitchens

*The clean painted surfaces and scrubbed boards of nautical style translate
perfectly to kitchen interiors, where shelves and cupboards keep crockery and
pots and pans shipshape, and flag-bright accessories give splashes of colour.*

TONGUE-AND-GROOVE BOARDING is a familiar
feature in seaside homes, and it makes an ideal
treatment for kitchen walls, wherever you live.
Boarding creates an interesting surface and also
has very good insulating properties. Painted a
soft white, it always looks clean and fresh.

Stone, tiled or wooden floors often prove the
most successful combination with all colours and
they can easily be mopped and wiped in case of
spillage. To soften hard surfaces, use rag rugs or
runners in colours that tie in with your kitchen.
Natural floor coverings fit well with seashore style
and there is a large choice available: coir, jute,
seagrass and sisal are all hardwearing. They can
either be cut to fit or made into mats bound with
coloured cotton tape.

Simple accessories, such as navy-and-white
striped dishtowels, give an instant nautical feel.
Kitchen shelves in naive style can be made using
reclaimed timber such as floorboards or driftwood,
colourwashed in off-white or chalky blue. Leave
kitchen windows unadorned and line windowsills
with displays of beautiful old model boats, seashells
and fresh herbs and flowers.

THIS PAGE, TOP A bowl filled with seashells collected
from the beach is one of the simplest ways to introduce
a breath of fresh seaside air into your kitchen.

OPPOSITE, CLOCKWISE FROM TOP LEFT This decoupage
tray with a marine theme is painted in the vibrant colours
of the Mediterranean and finished with chunky rope
handles. Display everyday china and glassware on a sturdy
kitchen dresser. Navy blue and white tiles make a stunning
background for no-fuss white metal kitchen goods.

Shoreline Dining

Sculptural driftwood, seedheads, pebbles, starfish and shells can be transformed into attractive and original table decorations. Their unadorned simplicity instils an air of tranquility – the perfect recipe for relaxed mealtimes.

CREATE ELEGANT TABLE SETTINGS by combining natural treasures with crisp plain linens, to set off their fabulous textures and subtle colours. Transform a linen cloth into a three-dimensional work of art by adorning it with tiny bundles of driftwood and delicately coloured shells. Attach the adornments to the hem using wire, so that they can be removed easily when the cloth needs washing.

Fine white china is beautiful in its own right, but if you are throwing a special dinner party, you might embellish each table setting with an individual maritime motif, or decorate china with small images of shells and starfish, using ceramic paint. Or fill a large glass dish with water, place white shells and stones at the bottom and float

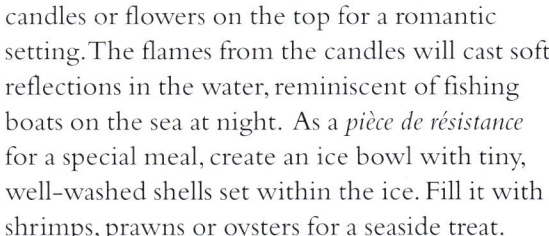

candles or flowers on the top for a romantic setting. The flames from the candles will cast soft reflections in the water, reminiscent of fishing boats on the sea at night. As a *pièce de résistance* for a special meal, create an ice bowl with tiny, well-washed shells set within the ice. Fill it with shrimps, prawns or oysters for a seaside treat.

THIS PAGE, CLOCKWISE FROM TOP LEFT Make beach-style settings by either wiring small shells on to the corners of napkins or tying napkins with ribbons decorated with shells or pebbles, glued or wired in place. Tiny bundles of driftwood bound with string, alternating with seashells, are attached with wire to the hem of this linen tablecloth.

OPPOSITE PAGE, TOP TO BOTTOM Delight your guests with personalized place markers, made by writing names on to smooth pebbles. Mix and match the colour tones and patterns of napkins for informal table settings.

Alfresco Eating

Long, lazy lunches or suppers are so much more pleasurable when set up outdoors, on a table laid with simple, unbreakable enamelware. Choose seaside shades of blues and aquas teamed with plenty of white to keep the look fresh.

BE PREPARED TO COPE WITH the elements when planning to eat in the open air. Table linens will need to be anchored down on breezy days, so scour the shoreline for attractive pebbles to keep napkins and placemats decoratively in place.

Add another dimension to a plain glass carafe by painting seaside motifs directly on to the glass. Use white glass paint to create the look of etched designs: seaweed, shells and starfish are all easy to master. Make a display of glassware, with a variety of glasses and pitchers in all shapes and sizes. For evening meals, the soft, warm glow of candlelight creates the perfect ambience. Group together old bottles found on the shore and place a candle in each. Tin lanterns add a gentle light and a magical atmosphere to informal suppers.

THIS PAGE, TOP TO BOTTOM
As a stunning centrepiece, wax-filled mussel shells used as candles are hard to beat. Use pebbles and feathers found on the beach as ornaments, and keep tableware simple to reflect the informal beachside look.

OPPOSITE PAGE
Blue and white are the classic seaside colours.

Nautical Living

COMMUNAL AREAS IN THE HOME need to be functional and inviting: harmonious, comfortable spaces that are the centre of family life. Used for relaxing, playing with the children, entertaining friends and perhaps for eating, they need to be adaptable and welcoming. White is the perfect foil for natural wood or painted furniture, and for evocative displays of seashore finds. If the room has a beautiful view, keep the decoration simple and the windows uncluttered.

ABOVE Smart buttoned cushions scattered casually throughout the room add a touch of relaxed comfort to the living room.

LEFT In this entrancing white-painted beach hut, the crisp striped canvas curtain hides deck chairs and other beach paraphernalia from view, to keep the small space uncluttered and welcoming.

Seashore Surfaces

Walls and floors form the shell of living spaces, and they need
to contribute to an atmosphere that is both harmonious and comforting.
The seashore theme can be used in many ways to achieve this effect.

ALONG THE SHORE, surfaces are bleached and distressed by salt spray, sun and wind. Wood and fabrics fade, metal rusts and paintwork peels to create subtle gradations of tone and texture.

Beach huts are the ultimate seashore dwellings. Sturdy bargeboarding outside and tongue-and-groove matchboarding inside create the snug atmosphere of a ship's cabin. Tongue-and-groove can be used on any dry wall to echo the look. Lighten floorboards with whitewash, or bleach and scrub them vigorously every time you clean them, or apply a coat of linseed oil mixed with white zinc pigment and seal with matt varnish.

Paint walls white or use pale washes in the colours of the sea to evoke an ocean mood. Experiment with textures – try applying paint with a sponge, cloth, wallpaper brush, bunch of long feathers or wide household brush. To add interest and depth, achieve a slightly rough plaster effect with a little plaster filler scraped over the surface. For a very subtle finish, the filler can be added to the paint and brushed over the wall.

THIS PAGE, TOP Tongue-and-groove cladding can help to give an informal beach-hut feel to interiors.

OPPOSITE PAGE, CLOCKWISE FROM TOP LEFT Add a nautical note to a plain wall, using rope applied in a wave design. Painting the rope the same colour as the wall will complete the finished look. For a Mediterranean theme, paint walls in a strong base colour, then wash over a darker tone. Bleached floorboards bring to mind scrubbed decks: team with wooden accessories to accentuate the effect. Lay a pattern of pebbles and stone tiles in a dry mix of sand and cement, then wet to set the mortar.

FLOOR-TO-CEILING WINDOWS create a link between this beautiful living room and the coastal waterway outdoors, establishing a sense of freedom and openness, which is so much a part of seashore style. The simple, relaxed furniture and the roof made of natural wood panelling help to maintain the comfortable ambience of the room.

Beachcomber's Furniture

Furniture made from seaworn driftwood can look elegant and timeless, and will fill your home with the reassuring calm inherent in untreated wood. This is a particularly creative way to give a personal look to interior furnishings.

THE SIMPLE ELEGANCE OF WOOD and whitewash is a timeless solution for seaside homes, where mismatched pieces of furniture work well against a backdrop of single-colour walls and flooring.

Rough wooden pallets come into their own – dismantle them and craft the slats into interesting tables, and pretty shelves. Even a grandfather clock can be made from odd pieces of wood, giving a new twist to a traditional look.

Search junkyards for interesting old furniture that can be renovated. Strip and sand the surface, then oil or wax the wood, or paint it in shades of sea-green, blue and soft red. To enliven tired old wicker furniture, paint it brilliant white to remind you of hot, sunny days on seashore verandahs.

THIS PAGE, TOP AND ABOVE Use reclaimed driftwood just as you find it – complete with stout nails sticking out. Clever ropework on a sofa adds an ocean theme.

OPPOSITE PAGE A low table and matching planter made from driftwood washed up on the beach; the wood bears the scars of its sea journey with pride.

Flotsam and Jetsam

Accessories form an integral part of interior design, so use them to reflect your personal tastes and surround yourself with things that make you happy. The scope for this style of decoration is boundless, and materials are plentiful and free.

GIVE DECORATIVE IDEAS a prominent place in your home and they will attract and hold the attention of your guests. Found objects can form an integral part of any display, whether they are the products of nature or reclaimed wood, rope or metal. Play colour against colour and texture against texture to maximize the effect.

Turn simple strips of driftwood into quirky candlesticks, and experiment with different arrangements and locations to keep the effect fresh, spontaneous and lively.

Natural treasures such as shells, starfish, stones and coral can be bought at craft and design stores but it is a shame to buy them when they are freely available. If you cannot find what you need on the beach, then use only those that you know to be the by-products of the fishing industry, such as mussel, scallop or oyster shells. Some shells on sale, those that are uniformly shiny and free from imperfections, will have been commercially harvested, a practice that is driving some seashore species to the verge of extinction.

THIS PAGE, TOP This doorstop is simplicity itself: a pile of smooth beach pebbles glued one on top of the other.

OPPOSITE PAGE, CLOCKWISE FROM TOP LEFT Take a tip from able-bodied seamen and create a stunning tie-back using rope tied with simple slip knots. Make a fireside alcove from wooden shelf edging, glued and coated with sand, and decorated with beach shells. Chunky twine and beads like fishing floats give cushions a contemporary edge. For a quick and easy blind, fringe the edge of a raffia beach mat. Add a piece of driftwood to make a blind pull, or thread shells on to wire for a more elaborate effect.

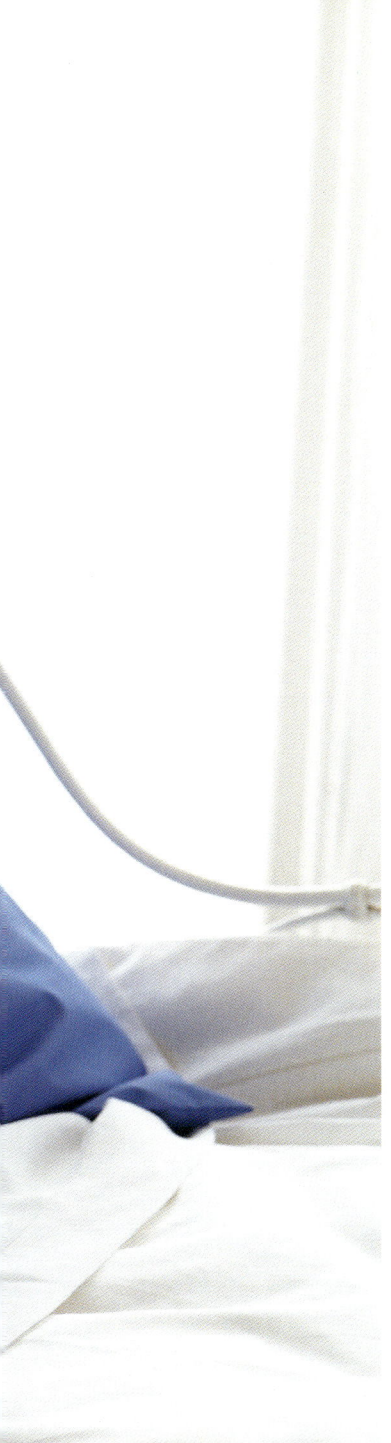

Sea Dreams

DECORATION IN THE BEDROOM should be tranquil and soothing. An all-white room is beautifully romantic, with crisp linens and fine voile curtains wafting in the sea breeze. Soft colours look glorious, too. Chalky lilacs and blues, aquas and delicate greens are all relaxing choices. Use softly distressed seaside colours on chests of drawers, wicker furniture and bed linen. Experiment with colour samples and watch what happens to them in different lights through the day.

ABOVE Use smooth beach pebbles to bring a quirky seaside style to a bedroom.

LEFT Fall asleep to the sound of the seashore in a fresh blue and white colour scheme, guaranteed to make you dream of clear skies and drifts of fluffy clouds. Chain-stitch embroidery using a single strand of thread gives a delicate feel to the marine decorations on the bed linen.

Sleeping Softly

*Of all the rooms in the house, the bedroom should be the most relaxing.
Shoreline finds, with their unique subtleties of texture and tone, can inspire
creative themes that will bring a sense of harmony to sleeping rooms.*

PLANKS OF RECLAIMED driftwood make rugged bedroom chairs and cupboards full of character. As well as searching the beach, hunt through junkyards for old wooden dressing tables, and for floorboards or pallets, which can be stripped and made into bed frames and headboards before being varnished or painted. Imitate the beautiful silvers and soft whites of aged, weatherworn wood with crackleglaze or by distressing existing modern bedheads.

Steamer trunks and wicker laundry hampers have an evocative seafaring charm and serve as flexible storage containers for bedding, blankets or toys. Transform a dull or damaged tabletop with a painted shell design, or collect real shells and use them to create a richly encrusted surface.

Authentic seashore-style chairs are those specifically designed for lazy days in the sun – wicker chairs, directors' chairs and, of course, traditional deck chairs with striped canvas.

THIS PAGE, TOP An old wooden pallet retains its naive roughness when transformed into a rustic headboard. Painting the wood a soft shade of white gives an end effect of harmony and tranquillity.

OPPOSITE PAGE, CLOCKWISE FROM TOP LEFT Driftwood forms a sturdy bedhead, and is decorated with pebbles and shells, lodged firmly in between its weathered planks. Create a vacation fantasy by suspending a calico canopy in the shape of a beach hut over seaside-striped bed linen. An ornate iron bedhead and a sea view make for a highly romantic bedroom setting. Beach mats are attached to the walls and ceiling here for a look that takes care of the styling of the whole bedroom in a single stroke, and is at the same time both light and clean.

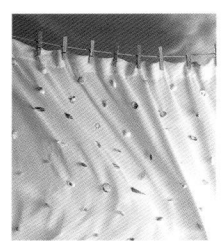

Sea-breeze Fabrics

The sound of fabric caught by the wind recalls sailing boats at sea or windsocks in a yacht marina. In summer, leave windows open to the sun and sky, and allow unlined curtains to blow free.

SEASHORE FABRICS FOR THE BEDROOM are best kept simple – natural linens, cottons and canvas, with stripes or checks to give bold accents of pattern. Lightweight cottons, voile and muslin will lift gently with the slightest breeze, and your spirits will lift with them. Translucent curtains can be softly swathed and edged with delicate shells. Modern fabrics incorporating natural fibres, such as hemp and raffia, also fit the seaside theme.

Nautical striped canvas curtains can be rigged up like sails, lashing the material on to a pole with a rope threaded through eyelets. Boating stores supply a huge range of ropes, pulleys and cleats that can be used to create an authentic nautical look. Thinking laterally, you can also use other items as poles, such as lengths of driftwood or

bamboo. Cushions, chair covers and throws provide instant warmth and comfort. For winter, add chunky woollen fabrics reminiscent of thick fisherman's sweaters. Deck-chair canvas can be used to cover cushions and directors' chairs.

THIS PAGE, TOP An elegant muslin curtain is dotted with shells, which have been attached with glue. The clothes pegs add to the open-air effect.

OPPOSITE PAGE, CLOCKWISE FROM TOP LEFT This bedroom throw was tie-dyed in a beautiful ocean blue colour, with embroidered cushion covers dyed to match. Dress up a plain linen curtain with a pretty shell edging; thread the shells on to wire first so that they are easy to remove when the curtain needs washing. Blue and white cottons are the essence of seashore style. Small checks mix well with other ginghams and stripes. Mosquito netting evokes a scene from tropical shores, wherever you live; stitch on starfish and seahorses for decoration.

All Aboard

Stamp your personality on a bedroom with pictures, flowers and objects you have kept as mementos of days by the sea. Even the most beautiful, serenely peaceful room can seem uninhabited until it is enlivened with decorative details that are special to you.

MOST OF US RETURN HOME from vacations or weekends away by the shore with pockets full of finds: satisfyingly smooth pebbles, shells and starfish, and jewel-like chunks of coloured glass, worn to a misty translucency by the relentless action of sea and sand.

Instead of simply discarding these mementos, you can easily incorporate them into your bedroom surroundings. Your initial spontaneous response to their natural beauty will inspire you to use them creatively in your decorative schemes. Scour the beach for interesting flotsam and jetsam – long after you return from the seashore, you can continue to enjoy their elemental qualities and associations as you drift off to sleep each night.

THIS PAGE, TOP TO BOTTOM Make simple curtains for a bedroom cabinet or window by stitching or glueing small knots of raffia and string, and small shells, on to white voile. The ever-popular sailing ship motif will add an instant seaside feel to a child's bedroom. A pair of bedroom slippers made from a soft natural waffle-weave cotton fabric epitomize the easy-going comfort that is so much a part of seashore style. The slippers have been customized with seashell embroidery – a novelty feature that will stir memories of summers by the beach, even on the darkest of winter days.

OPPOSITE PAGE, TOP TO BOTTOM Give your bedroom cushions a bold nautical look by covering them in white and dark blue felt. Make holes at regular intervals around the edges, using a hole punch, then insert brass rivets and thread with white cord or rope. A linen laundry bag is a practical bedroom accessory and it adds an elegant seaside theme. This bag has been finished off very simply, with a drawstring trimmed with seashells, but adding seaside motifs to the fabric would be just as effective.

BLUE AND WHITE LINEN or cotton dishtowels combine the crispness and softness of natural fabrics with a colour scheme that is instantly evocative of the seaside. While their design is utterly traditional it always looks fresh and appealing.

Here, dishtowels have been transformed into a wonderfully comfortable padded seat cushion that would work well in any bedroom setting, and especially as part of a window seat offering uninterrupted sea views. The dishtowels have been quilted using a technique that is employed in many countries, such as Greece, where mattresses are stuffed with cotton or natural horsehair. Polyester wadding, or batting, provides a cheaper alternative that is just as effective and is also lightweight and washable.

Seawater Worlds

BATHROOMS, ALTHOUGH FUNCTIONAL, can also be leisurely and luxurious rooms – somewhere to unwind and soak away your cares after a hard day. The watery bathroom world is the ideal place to introduce a seashore theme. Shell collections and arrangements of sea sponge and coral can be used to decorate shelves; towels and shower curtains can be painted or embroidered with seascape motifs. Add a chair and make the bathroom a place to linger in.

ABOVE Mosaic tiling in seascape colours fits easily into a bathroom scheme.

LEFT A cupboard makes a practical fixture for a bathroom wall, and one made from sea-weathered wood will also add plenty of character to the room. This cupboard is made from planks of driftwood, and uses two pairs of scallop shells to conceal the hinges.

Shipshape Surfaces

Seashore style is naturally at home in the bathroom, where water is the dominant element, and the emphasis is on waterproof surfaces, clean lines and compact, efficient storage. A nautical theme springs instantly to mind.

APPLY THE SEASHORE THEME to bathroom doors, shutters or furniture in the form of sun-bleached paintwork. Stack old tea chests, open ends facing out, to make an instant storage unit, or turn them upside down for a makeshift table. In addition, you can use their wood to craft a small cupboard. Rustic shelves can be created from cast-off pallets or crates; the charm of these shelves is their naive quality, so rough or uneven edges are part of the effect. Colourwash the shelves in strong Mediterranean or Pacific shades, or try a soft grey-blue for the sophisticated look of the American east coast.

Duckboarding brings to mind boats, marinas and indulgent days spent beside a pool. If you are feeling adventurous you could create a whole duckboard floor, positioning the slats close together. Not only would this make an original surface, but stepping out of the bath or shower on to the smooth wood would always be a treat.

THIS PAGE, TOP A little boat to float in the bath is an essential bathroom accessory for children of all ages.

OPPOSITE PAGE, CLOCKWISE FROM TOP LEFT These charming rustic shelves have been handcrafted from a recycled wooden pallet; pallets can be picked up cheaply or even free from junkyards, warehouses or foodstores, and painting them white gives them a new lease of life. Crackleglaze is an excellent medium for ageing new doors and shutters; the porthole window, seen here, completes the nautical look. A duckboard mat made from hardwood slats is practical for use in the shower or as a bath mat. A mosaic design makes a highly sophisticated alternative to tiles as a splashback on the walls around the bath or in the base of the shower.

Shoreline Treasures

Take a stroll along the beach and draw your inspiration from nature's treasures at the water's edge. Use the colours, textures and natural gifts of the sea as creative themes for beautifying your bathroom.

DECORATIVE IDEAS with a seashore theme can be crafted from everyday objects already in use in your bathroom. For example, a simple wooden storage box could be painted and decorated with a cornucopia of shells, and a glass vase could be turned into a display case filled to overflowing with seashore finds.

Seashore treasures are the perfect foil in this watery world, and they help to give your bath and shower rooms a refreshing feel of the great outdoors. Arrange shells along the windowsill so that they catch the sunlight, and fill shelves with displays of coral and other mementos of days at the coast. Create a chair rail using strips of rope with shells and pebbles attached, or add a simple decorative line of clam shells around the wall. If you want to go overboard, you could cover

the walls from ceiling to floor with shells and pebbles set into plaster, turning your bathroom into a magical underwater grotto.

One unique way to display seashore finds is to make a screen to hang from a window. Attach sea-worn fragments of glass, shells, stones, and fishing floats on to a length of near-visible fishing line. The screen will appear to float in mid-air and the more you gaze at it, the more the image of the sea comes to mind.

THIS PAGE, CLOCKWISE FROM TOP LEFT Relax at the end of a hard day in a bath lit by candles – anchor them in a box of pebbles, or fill a collection of open shells with small nightlights. Calico sails adorn this yacht, which has been constructed from well-chosen pieces of driftwood found on the beach. The bathroom is the ideal place to display starfish, sea sponge, pebbles and other rock pool finds.

OPPOSITE PAGE, TOP TO BOTTOM The beauty of this scallop shell sconce lies in its simplicity. The candle light radiates along the grooves of the shell, and creates an atmosphere of peaceful serenity. Complement the freshness of your seashore bathroom with a basket of seashells and accessories made from natural materials, such as cotton and wicker.

Life on the Ocean Wave

*Give your bathroom the feel of the watery deep by adding decorative designs to key features.
Choose motifs to complement your bathroom décor and pick a co-ordinating colour scheme,
from crisp monochrome to candy-coloured pastels or strong, bright Mediterranean colours.*

WHILE THE BATHROOM is the ideal place to display a collection of shells and other seaside finds, you can also extend the marine theme to decorative details on walls, floors and bathroom accessories such as mirrors, towels and ceramics.

Simple shell and fish motifs lend themselves happily to mosaic, using subtle blends of blues, greens and whites to achieve a watery effect. You could use the same technique to decorate a mirror frame or table. If you are feeling confident, a mosaic floor in a wave or spiral shell design would complete a Mediterranean room scheme in a sumptuous, highly elegant style.

Give your shower room all the freshness of the outdoors with motifs inspired by the beach. A clear shower curtain provides a perfect backdrop on which you can create your own seaside mood with whatever designs you choose. Starfish, seahorses, shells and seaweed, applied in waterproof paint, will sway gently, as though rocked by an ocean current.

THIS PAGE, TOP Seek out beautifully decorated urns, jars and storage containers on a fishy theme.

OPPOSITE PAGE, CLOCKWISE FROM TOP LEFT A mosaic mirror makes a decorative focal point in the bathroom, and can be used to add accents of strong colour to a neutral colour scheme. Use decoupage to add seashore designs to bathroom accessories if you prefer not to draw motifs freehand. Add some delicate pastel colour to an all-white bathroom with a repeated pattern of seashore motifs painted on to a shower curtain; a set of bathroom towels could be embroidered to match. Paint a clear shower curtain with a selection of randomly scattered motifs in crisp white.

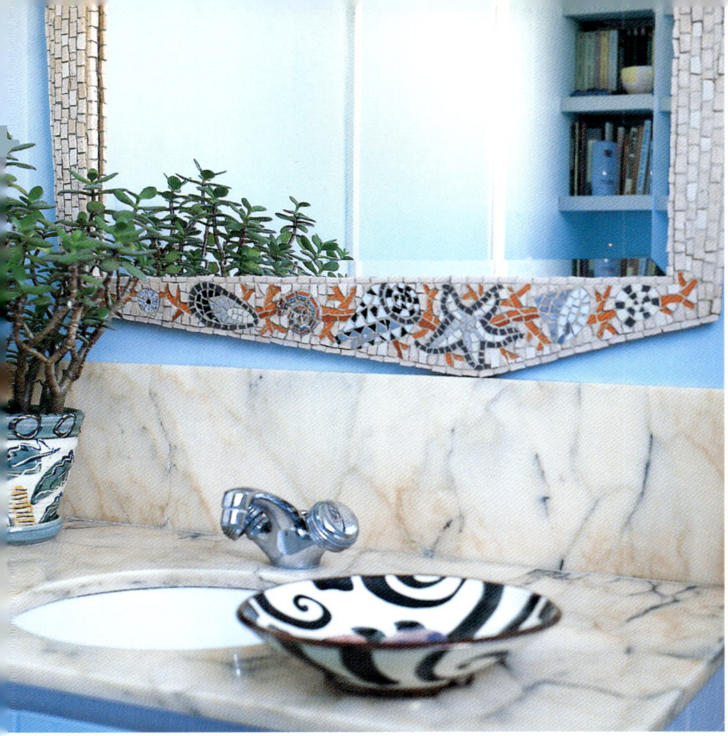

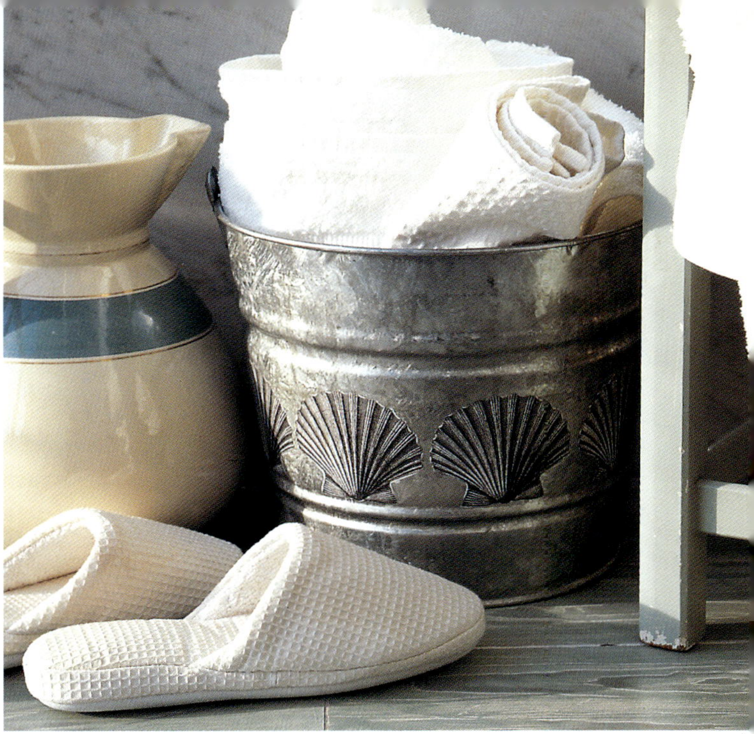

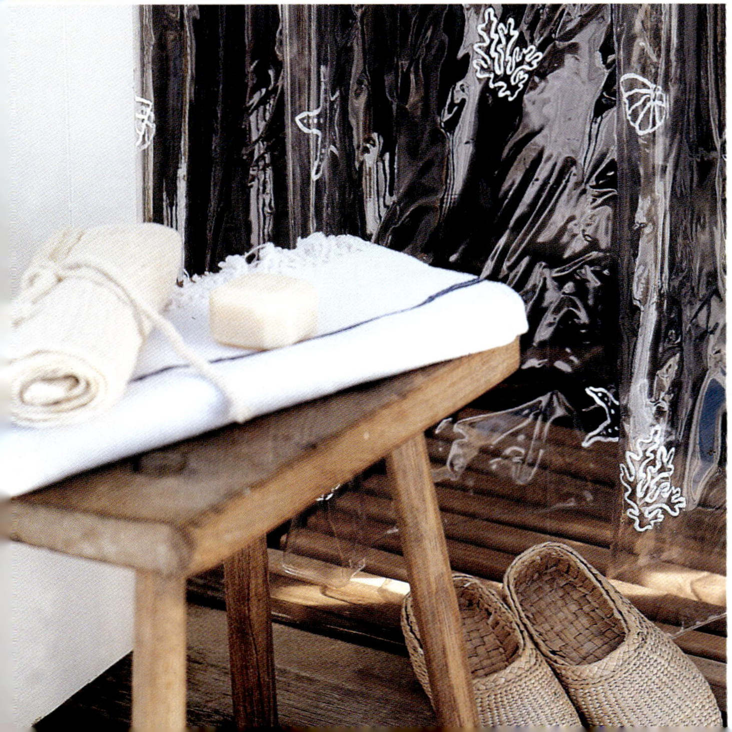

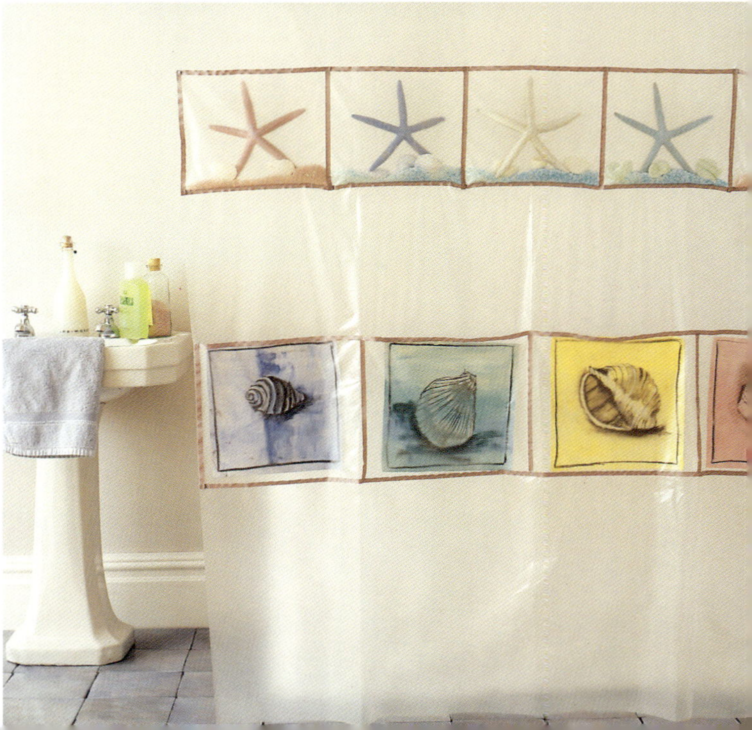

Seashore Adornments

IN A SIMPLE INTERIOR, details add a personal note and breathe life into a room. Make the most of *objets trouvés* brought back from the seaside by putting them on display around the house. The essence of seashore style is its uncomplicated approach, so keep arrangements informal. The sculptural shapes of driftwood appear functional and modern, while the roughness of rope, jute and raffia lends a texture that is reminiscent of ships and the sea.

ABOVE Arrange seashells and other finds on a windowsill to catch the light.

LEFT Weathered driftwood, sometimes with traces of ancient paint still adhering to its surface, can be fashioned into shelves, frames, trays or boxes. Hang mirrors and pictures in driftwood frames from lengths of bleached rope to continue the beachcombing theme throughout your home.

Maritime Displays

The delight of discovery is one of life's most enduring pleasures, and it gives found objects a special meaning. Create a series of still-life effects by arranging collections of your favourite mementos, unified by colour and theme.

REMEMBERING ON WHICH BEACH and on what occasion you unearthed your prize enhances the delight you feel when you see it as part of an ornamental display. Let the beach finds themselves be your inspiration. The idea is to celebrate the natural beauty of what you have collected, so look closely at shape, colour and texture. Early spring is one of the best times to comb the beach for treasures, on a morning following a stormy night, when the winds and violent seas of winter have brought up the most bounty.

THIS PAGE, TOP TO BOTTOM Group pebbles and shells and illuminate them with flickering candles. An armful of driftwood takes on a sculptural quality.

OPPOSITE PAGE Make a feature of pieces of translucent sea-worn glass, strung together in a jewel-like garland.

Cast-adrift Frames

Decorate interior walls with ornamental frames constructed from seaside finds.
You can dress up old mirror or picture frames and create your very own works of art —
you don't even need to be able to draw.

FINDING INSPIRATION FOR your frames is largely just a matter of scouring the beach or shoreline for interesting pebbles, seaweed, shells and pieces of driftwood. Searching for driftwood is a particular pleasure, as the pieces are often sculpted by the sea into fascinating shapes. Sea-weathered driftwood frames, or painted wood frames distressed with crackleglaze, can be as beautiful to look at as the images within them.

You might find wood that shows traces of faded paintwork or lettering, hinting at its previous life. Such details add character to the frame, and might give you a theme for the image to put inside it.

A plain wooden picture frame is also typical of the uncluttered approach that is seashore style: sand off old layers of varnish and bleach the wood,

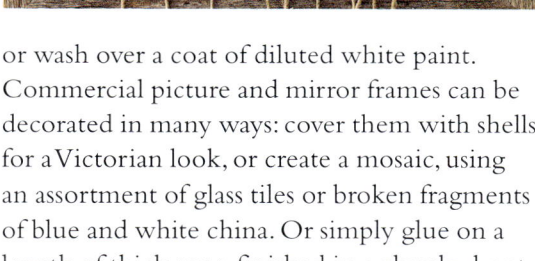

or wash over a coat of diluted white paint. Commercial picture and mirror frames can be decorated in many ways: cover them with shells for a Victorian look, or create a mosaic, using an assortment of glass tiles or broken fragments of blue and white china. Or simply glue on a length of thick rope, finished in a chunky knot.

THIS PAGE, CLOCKWISE FROM TOP LEFT This recycled frame has the weathered, grey tones of driftwood; the little boat is simply an aptly shaped pebble with sails torn from a fibre plant pot, and the string binding reinforces the seashore theme. For a stunningly simple mirror frame, glue assorted seashore finds on to an existing wooden frame, or go one step further by framing a mirror yourself with lengths of sanded-down driftwood found on the beach. A shell-encrusted mirror has an enchanting grotto-like feel: the larger the mirror, the more effective the look.

OPPOSITE PAGE, TOP TO BOTTOM Mosaic is the perfect material with which to frame a small mirror; the blue glass will remind you of seawater sparkling in bright summer sunlight. This frame was created from flat pieces of driftwood glued together very simply; the addition of limpet shells as a finishing touch evokes folktales of ancient shipwrecks.

Fun on the Beach

Holiday outings to the beach are all about having fun. Gifts and games inspired by the seashore share that carefree quality and conjure up memories of idyllic summer experiences of warm sand and sea breezes.

YOU CAN SHARE THE PLEASURE you take in your natural trophies from the seashore by using them to make beautiful, original gifts for family and friends. Seashells and small pieces of driftwood can be used to add trimmings to gift wraps, too.

It's easy to turn a simple wooden box into a special gift with the addition of a design worked in pretty shells: just choose a selection of well-shaped shells to suit your box, arrange them as you please and glue them in place. Children can help you gather bucketfuls of small shells so that you have a good selection to choose from.

There are few things more flattering than receiving notepaper, cards and stationery crafted by hand. Buy beautifully textured handmade paper to suit the natural theme. Decorating it is easy,

using all manner of beach and rock pool treasures, such as seashells, feathers, pebbles, seaweed, and sprinklings of sand and shingle. There are no end of motifs and designs to bring the seaside to mind if you really want to get creative.

THIS PAGE, TOP Stitch rows of small shells around a rattan basket for a beautiful contrast of textures.

OPPOSITE PAGE, CLOCKWISE FROM TOP LEFT A duffel bag is reminiscent of seafaring folk setting sail for distant lands; this hardwearing white cotton drill duffel bag is decorated at the knot with a small piece of driftwood. Glueing small pieces of string and driftwood on to quality writing paper creates a personalized gift that will always be well received. A straw hat is the perfect accessory for children on the beach in summer; they will get even more pleasure from it if they have collected the shells and feathers themselves. Gift-wrap presents in fabric bags tied with string and decorated with shells and driftwood.

IN KEEPING WITH the playful spirit of the seaside, you can use a collection of beach pebbles to create a novel version of the game of dominoes. Children and adults alike will enjoy searching the coastline for smooth pebbles of a uniform size and shape. Choose reasonably small pebbles, or the whole set will be very heavy. The spots can then be drawn on using a fine-tipped permanent marker. Play with them on the beach, or take them home as a reminder of the day.

If you want, make a suitable bag to keep the dominoes in. Choose a natural material that suits their weight. Sacking has a wonderful tactile quality, and it is also hardwearing and inexpensive. Make your own drawstring bag, using a tapestry needle and a few sacking threads pulled from the raw edges to stitch the side seams. Near the top edge, thread through a length of jute twine for the drawstring. Bind a few shells to the twine to complete the effect.

Outdoor Seascapes

EVEN THE SMALLEST and most urban of garden spaces can be transformed into an ocean vista. Go for the windswept look and avoid straight lines and regularly shaped beds, which would look unnatural. Use furnishings in your garden in the same way as you would use them inside the house, and see how easy it is to invoke the spirit of the sea. Collect exciting flotsam and jetsam, washed ashore, and give them a new lease of life, recycled in the seaside garden.

ABOVE A still life of rowing oars and a garland strung with pebbles sets an evocative scene against panelled wooden garden fencing.

LEFT This fishing harbour is surrounded by beautifully soft seascape scenery. While few of us are lucky enough to live with views of this sort, we can all take inspiration from sights enjoyed on trips away from home.

Seashore Gardens

The wild plants of coastal regions are tough survivors. Living on exposed hillsides and cliff faces, they have to endure fierce gales and salt spray. These hardy plants need very little attention, and they will give a natural, untamed feel to the most urban of gardens.

PLANTING CHOICES FOR SEASHORE gardens should reflect the wild, windswept shoreline. Choose grasses, varying from short tufts to tall, sweeping swathes, and don't try to achieve anything more than an informal garden design. Rosemary, a typical seashore plant, can be used alongside other herbs to add fragrance to the garden, while geraniums and pelargoniums will add welcome splashes of vivid colour.

THIS PAGE, TOP TO BOTTOM Tiny saxifrages contrast with the pebbles and pinks. Typically hardy plants suggest coastal flora, and by planting them in a rock garden you can recreate a craggy seaside habitat. Add extra touches of seashore style using scallop shells as decoration.

OPPOSITE PAGE A mosaic of blue glazed tiles highlights the maritime theme suggested by the sea-washed stones and spiky planting. The rowing boat adds to the effect.

Sea-washed Furniture

Take your seashore style outdoors with a few well-chosen pieces of garden furniture.
Choose natural materials, such as wicker, canvas and painted or sun-bleached wood,
to evoke the faded charm of a seaside terrace.

FURNITURE OFFERS PLENTY of scope for decoration and adds structural definition to your garden and outdoor spaces. Tables and comfortable chairs are also a practical necessity if you want to use your garden as a vibrant living area in which to eat, relax and entertain friends.

Folding directors' chairs make convenient occasional summer seating, their canvas covers and wooden frames recalling the traditional deck chair of the seaside. Wicker armchairs acquire a wonderful lived-in look when they have been weathered by the sun. Add a few plump cushions to make them even more comfortable.

Living outside sometimes requires shelter and shade from the wind or from the blistering sun. A windbreak will allow you to sit outside in breezy weather, while a large parasol will provide shade from the midday sun in high summer; these pieces are familiar sights on the beach and they will tie in perfectly with the seashore theme.

THIS PAGE, TOP Paint an old slatted wooden chair in contrasting stripes for a traditional seaside look.

OPPOSITE PAGE, CLOCKWISE FROM TOP LEFT Here, a simple wooden chair has been transformed into nautical seating by binding the legs and back with a length of garden string; awkward seams are decorated with pieces of flotsam and jetsam as a finishing touch. The faded canvas stripes of a deck chair recall memories of childhood holidays at the seaside. A mosaic table is a practical addition and provides a stunning focal point for the garden. The cleverly co-ordinated shades of blue and green evoke fresh breezes sweeping in off the water. Provided you keep to a simple shape and design, you will find the process of creating mosaic very simple.

Nautical Accessories

Adding characterful ornaments to exterior walls and surfaces gives the garden
a lived-in feel, and adds personality and charm to outdoor spaces. For an authentic
seashore style, the elements should look effortlessly arranged.

THE MOST BASIC GARDEN DETAILS will have impact if your decorative ideas have novelty value. An afternoon spent trawling the shoreline can throw up all kinds of material to be fashioned into sea-themed accessories. Found objects can make wonderful informal sculptures: prop a life belt against a garden chair or drape fishing nets over a boundary wall to add a touch of the unexpected.

For more elaborate displays, build a sand garden with a frame of reclaimed wood; arrange shells, coral and cork in the sand, and surround it with typical seaside plants to complete the look. If you want to get really creative, craft a sailing boat from driftwood, turn lobster pots into plant containers, or embellish plant pots with necklaces made from seashells glued on in a zigzag design.

Giving a twist to existing garden features can be just as effective as creating displays and artefacts. Turn a shed into a beach hut by painting it in ice cream colours, or add motifs to gateposts and driveways. Conjure up the expansive freedom of the ocean and the taste of fresh sea air with wind chimes that tinkle softly in the breeze.

THIS PAGE, TOP A rusty anchor chain twisted around a plant container makes an original garden feature.

OPPOSITE PAGE, CLOCKWISE FROM TOP LEFT A wreath made from rope and embellished with shells and ribbon makes a striking detail against a painted wooden door. Hang a seashell mobile from an open window to catch the breeze and make gentle sounds reminiscent of the sea. A sailor's hammock, together with marine-coloured glass balls, provides a place to dream of adventures on the high seas. Seashells decorate this beach hut-style birdhouse.

Index